oremus

A Guide to Catholic Prayer

Leader's Guide

Fr. Mark Toups

Ascension Press
West Chester, Pennsylvania

Oremus is an adult faith formation resource of Ascension Press.

Ascension Press
Post Office Box 1990
West Chester, PA 19380
Customer service: 1-800-376-0520
AscensionPress.com

Cover design: Devin Schadt

Printed in the United States of America

ISBN 978-1-935940-47-0

Contents

Student Workbook Contents

PRAYER FOR LEADERS AND FACILITATORS

Father, I abandon myself into your hands;
do with me what you will.
Whatever you may do,
I shall always thank you.
I am ready for all, I accept all;
let only your will be done in me,
and in all your creatures;
no more do I wish than this, O Lord.
Into your hands I commend my soul.
I offer it to you with all the love of my heart,
for I love you, Lord,
and so need to give myself,
to surrender myself into your hands without reserve,
and with boundless confidence,
for you are my Father.
–Brother Charles of Jesus (Charles de Foucauld)

A Letter to Leaders and Facilitators from Fr. Mark Toups

Dear Leaders and Facilitators,

Thank you for agreeing to serve as a facilitator for *Oremus*. Over the next eight weeks you will have the privilege of praying for, and praying with, the men and women God will bring to you. As God has called you to serve, allow me to share a few encouragements.

Throughout *Oremus* you will hear me repeatedly quote the *Catechism of the Catholic Church*, "*God calls man first.* … the living and true God tirelessly calls each person to that mysterious encounter known as prayer. In prayer, the faithful God's initiative of love always comes first; our own first step is always a response."[1] As you lead, I invite you to follow. Remember, "*God's initiative of love always comes first.*" Trust that God *is* active; all you have to do is watch what God is doing.

Pope Benedict XVI reminded us, "God looks after me. … He is not a distant God."[2] The Holy Father also teaches us that God "loves with a personal love."[3] While God the Father loves all humanity, his love is particular and personal. He is not a distant Father. He is a Father who gazes upon us and does so with a particular, personal gaze. "God is looking at us. Not in general, not in principle, not in the abstract—but here and now and specifically."[4]

I encourage you to embrace the dynamic that each person will have a uniquely personal experience of *Oremus*. Many will experience God like never before. Others may feel as if the examples and stories name their own experience. Still others may struggle and compare their prayer with the prayer of others in the class. I encourage you to encourage them. Because prayer is personal, *Oremus* will be different for everyone.

Pope Benedict XVI also states, "The proclamation of and *witness* to the Gospel are the first service that Christians can render to every person and the entire human race, called as they are to communicate to all God's love, which was fully manifested in Jesus Christ, the one Redeemer of the world."[5] As a facilitator you are called to teach and *witness*. I encourage you to embrace *Oremus* as a personal pilgrimage, one that requires you to lead from your own experience of prayer rather than from techniques or coaching. You must be praying if you are going to lead others in prayer. I have learned this as a teacher; we teach best from what we have learned as students.

Again, thank you for your "yes." God can do much with our littleness. Trust in God's initiative. Expect him to work miracles. Watch for what he is doing.

Let's pray for each other.

In Christ,

Fr. Mark Toups

Fr. Mark Toups

---

1. *Catechism of the Catholic Church*, 2567.
2. Homily on Solemnity of the Sacred Heart of Jesus, June 11, 2010.
3. *Deus Caritas Est*, 9.
4. Robert R. Marsh, SJ. "Looking at God Looking at You," *The Way*, 43/4 (October 2004), 28.
5. Pope Benedict XVI, 40th Anniversary of Vatican II's *Ad gentes*, March 11, 2006, 334.

Leader's Overview

About the *Oremus* Program

Oremus \ō-'rā-müs\ which is Latin for "Let us pray," is a Catholic adult faith formation program that seeks to help people learn how to pray within the Tradition of the Catholic Church. Each session focuses on a related group of topics that sequentially teaches the essential basics of prayer.

Each lesson in *Oremus* involves an informative and inspiring DVD presentation by Fr. Mark Toups, followed by a small-group discussion of the truths he presented in that lesson, many of which are derived from principles contained in the "Spiritual Exercises" of St. Ignatius of Loyola. Participants are invited to pray between sessions with specific Scripture passages provided in the Student Workbook. They are also encouraged to write down their prayer experiences in a journal section provided in the Workbook. *Oremus* teaches participants how to pray, leading them through an eight-week retreat in the midst of their busy lives.

The primary goal of *Oremus* is to help people deepen their relationship with God so that our parishes become, in the words of Blessed John Paul II, "schools of prayer" (see *Novo Millennio Ineunte* #33). Each session provides multiple opportunities to achieve this goal with instruction, practical examples, and small-group discussion, all followed by personal prayer.

Resources and Tips to Help You Plan

The following checklist may be useful in helping you to organize your study:

1. Thoroughly familiarize yourself with the course materials before you begin.

2. Schedule eight ninety-minute sessions as far in advance as possible. Put them on the parish calendar so that no other events will be planned for the same times.

3. Decide on your promotional plan and budget.

4. Depending on the size of your group, you may want to consider forming a Study Group Team to assist you in planning and executing the study. Some possible roles for which you may decide to recruit people include:

   - *Publicity Coordinator* – to assist in promoting the study
   - *Registration Coordinator* – to coordinate the registration process
   - *Hospitality Coordinator* – to handle greeters and refreshments
   - *Facilities Coordinator* – to handle the opening and closing of the venue at which you will meet and to arrange for chairs, tables, and audiovisual equipment
   - *Prayer Coordinator* – to devise and implement a prayer plan for spiritual support of the study group

5. Several weeks prior to the study, begin recruiting group discussion facilitators. You will need one facilitator for each group of six to eight students. For more details, see "Recruiting and Training Group Discussion Facilitators" (L-vi).

6. Set up registration far enough in advance to allow you to order and receive the Student Workbooks, as well as any other study supplies you need. A registration deadline of two weeks before the start date tends to work well. (We suggest that you order materials for an additional ten percent above your preregistered number to have on hand for last-minute registrants. You can return any materials in good condition that you don't use.)

7. Once you know how many people will be attending the study, arrange for an appropriate meeting space and for the audiovisual equipment and other supplies you will need. Some parishes choose to have Bibles available for those who would like to use them. Consider having a hospitality table with simple refreshments, which may help to break the ice and foster discussion within the group.

8. Schedule a ninety-minute Facilitator Orientation Meeting about two weeks (and no later than one week) prior to the start date. For more details, see "Recruiting and Training Group Discussion Facilitators."

9. Arrive early for the first session to set up the registration table and hospitality area and to arrange the gathering areas for the audiovisual presentation and discussion.

10. Pray for God's blessing on the study, asking that he will use it to work in the lives of the participants.

If you have any questions or concerns about preparing for this study, feel free to call and speak with a knowledgeable Ascension Press Study Consultant at 1-800-376-0520.

Effective Ways to Increase Attendance

Two to Three Months Before Your Study Begins

- Hang promotional posters around your parish (e.g., church common areas, parish school, Knights of Columbus halls). Downloadable posters are available at AscensionPress.com.

- Announce the study on your parish website and enter the dates on your parish calendar. Embed the *Oremus* highlight video available at AscensionPress.com on your parish website.

- Inform and involve other ministry leaders (e.g., Bible study group leaders, Knights of Columbus officers, seniors group leaders, and school parents). Let them know about your study and invite them to encourage their groups to attend, or run the same study for their group at a different time so you can share the DVDs.

- Submit an article or announcement to your parish, school newsletter, or Facebook page.

- Place an announcement or ad in your diocesan and local secular newspapers. They are often free.

- Run free community calendar announcements on Catholic or secular radio stations.

- Invite neighboring parishes to attend. Ask them to place an announcement in their bulletins and post flyers around their parish.

Four to Six Weeks Before Your Study Begins

- Place an announcement in your parish bulletin. Announcements should run through the registration deadline and continue until the study begins. Sample announcements are available at AscensionPress.com.

- Ask your pastor to announce your *Oremus* study at weekend Masses and encourage participation. A pastor's direct invitation is very effective. Invite people to register after Mass. Have a sample lesson playing for people to view at the registration table.

- That same week, insert flyers in your parish bulletin or stack them alongside several sample workbooks on registration tables at the back of church. Have people available at the tables to answer questions. Downloadable flyers are available at AscensionPress.com.

- Commission a group of five to ten "inviters" to personally invite people they know and encourage attendance. A personal invitation is always very effective.

- Ask participants to bring at least one friend with them.

- Allow late registrations, even after the study has begun.

Registration and Ordering Materials

Most parishes begin the registration process for their study at least four to six weeks in advance of the start date. Order your materials far enough in advance to ensure that you will have them on hand for the first session. Call an Ascension Press Study Consultant at 1-800-376-0520 to discuss or place your order.

You will need the following materials on hand for your *Oremus* study:

- ***Oremus* DVD Set.** Eight thirty-minute presentations by Fr. Mark Toups. (The sessions are also available on audio CDs.)

- ***Oremus* Leader's Guide.** Additional resources, including an orientation video for leaders and facilitators, can be found at AscensionPress.com.

- ***Oremus* Student Workbook.** Includes session outlines, group discussion questions, a journal section and more. Order one for each participant.

- **Bible.** Students will use Scripture verses during their at-home prayer time. A Catholic version is recommended. We offer bulk discounts on the Revised Standard Version-Catholic Edition, along with helpful Bible Tabs and other resources to assist with locating the book and verse.

- **Optional:** Extra DVD or CD set(s) for lending library. (Additional sets are helpful for leaders and facilitators to prepare for lessons and to loan out for those who miss a session.)

When you order materials, as noted above, *be sure to order extra copies of the Student Workbooks to have on hand for latecomers.* We suggest adding 10 percent to the number of preregistered students. You can return the materials you don't use. You may order your materials by calling 1-800-376-0520 or online at AscensionPress.com, if you have already spoken with a Study Consultant.

Recruiting and Training Group Discussion Facilitators

Group discussions are an integral part of the *Oremus* study—and facilitators play an essential role in fostering successful and fruitful group discussions!

Facilitators do not have to be experts in prayer or theology. Choose individuals who have a knack for making others feel welcome and who are able to draw out those who need a little extra encouragement. (It is also important that they have the ability to play "traffic cop," reining in more exuberant participants.)

You will want to have at least one facilitator for every six to eight participants, with possibly a few extra hands to fill in as needed.

About two weeks before the first session, schedule a ninety-minute Facilitator Orientation Meeting. Begin by showing the "Leader's Introduction" video, which is included as a special feature on the *Oremus* DVD set and is also available at AscensionPress.com. Then go over the materials and preview the first week's presentation and discussion questions. Be sure to begin and end the meeting with prayer, and encourage your facilitators to make prayer the foundation of their planning and preparation.

The next section is written especially for facilitators and is also available as a download at AscensionPress.com. Be sure that all facilitators get a copy and review it with your group at the Facilitator Training Session.

Group Discussion Facilitator's Guidelines

Remember, the role of a facilitator is not to teach—or even to answer questions—but rather, to welcome group members and guide them through the lesson, aiming to give everyone a chance to participate. *The facilitator does not make a discussion good; he or she makes a good discussion possible.*

Preparing for Each Session

Before each session, review the session outlines in the Student Workbook. This will give you a general overview of the themes that Fr. Toups will present. Also read through the Discussion Questions and spend some time considering how people may respond to them. This will help you to be prepared for some of the paths the discussion may take. Some facilitators may choose to preview the DVD or CD presentation ahead of time, but this is not required.

The most important preparation for you as a facilitator is to go through the study yourself. Be sure to spend time looking over the weekly prayer and journaling assignments. Your personal participation in the study will help you relate to and understand the experiences of your group members.

Tips for Managing Your Group

The facilitator's role is crucial to the success of the study. Remember, it is not the facilitator's job to answer every question that comes up; in fact, *a facilitator should answer a question only if no one else will answer or after everyone has spoken*. Whenever possible, he or she should attempt to point the participants toward a response instead of giving one directly. Here are a few other tips to help you guide your group in a fruitful, enjoyable discussion.

- **Set the right tone** from the beginning. Be welcoming and enthusiastic. Explain that group discussion helps clarify and fill in gaps that participants may have missed in the presentation, allows them to share what they have learned, and prepares them to go deeper. Your goal will be to spend sufficient time on each question to do those things.

- **Stay on time and on topic.** Some find it helpful to have a second person in the group who is responsible for giving them a ten-minute "warning" signal, to allow ample time to finish the discussion and close with prayer. You may also want to note the halfway point of your discussion period, and mark the question you would like to have reached five or ten minutes before the end of the session. Finishing the discussion period (and the session) promptly is essential and shows respect for your students' time. Losing the confidence of students through late wrap-ups may discourage them from coming back or from signing up for future studies.

- **Take control.** You are the discussion leader; the group will expect you to keep the discussion moving along:
    - † Watch for clues that a timid person has something to say, and encourage that person without putting him or her on the spot.
    - † Kindly "rein in" any participants who dominate the group so that others have a chance to speak. If they continue, ask them privately to help you get others to participate.
    - † Gently redirect tangential remarks or questions.
- **Remind the group of the "ABCs of Good Group Discussion":** *Be audible, brief, and Christ-centered …* and don't *"double dip"*! (That is, those who have had a chance to share should hold back until others have had a chance.)
- **Don't be afraid of silence**—but don't let it continue too long.

TEN COMMANDMENTS

FOR GREAT SMALL-GROUP DISCUSSIONS

1. **Be prepared.**
2. **Come on time.**
3. **If you did not prepare, allow others to speak before you do.**
4. **Listen to others.**
5. **Stick to the topic and questions at hand.**
6. **Never ridicule or cut down another's answer.**
7. **When you disagree, do so with respect and charity.**
8. **Don't fear silence.**
9. **Don't share confidences outside the group.**
10. **Enjoy yourself!**

SESSION OVERVIEW

How to Structure Each Session

Allow ninety minutes for each session to ensure sufficient time for participants to gather, view the DVD presentation, engage in small group discussion, and conclude the session. A short break should also be provided. Here is a sample agenda:

- **Introduction** (5 to 10 minutes)

  Gathering and opening remarks

- **View DVD presentation** (30 minutes)

  A thirty-minute talk by Fr. Mark Toups provides the welcome and opening prayer, reviews the previous week's lesson, provides spiritual direction and encouragements, and presents the topic.

- **Small-Group Discussion** (45 minutes)

  After the presentation, each session concludes with a forty-five-minute small-group discussion. Facilitators lead participants through a discussion of the topic at hand, as well as through general reflections about their growth in prayer.

- **Closing** (5 to 10 minutes)

  Closing remarks and prayer

Prayer and Journaling

In between group sessions, the journaling section in the *Oremus* Student Workbook guides participants through 20 to 25 minutes of prayerful reading and reflection each day, based on a Scripture passage related to the topic at hand. The journal questions (to be filled in after their prayer) help participants to notice what happened during prayer so that they become more aware of God "speaking" to their hearts through Scripture and through the inner promptings of the Holy Spirit. As they become familiar with these movements, participants may soon grow in awareness of God's presence in other aspects of their lives as well. Over the course of the program, participants will be drawn into a deeper relationship with God through a deeper understanding and practice of *lectio divina* and relational (imaginative) prayer.

FOR MORE INFORMATION

Please visit AscensionPress.com for helpful information regarding *Oremus* and for free downloadable resources. If you have any questions regarding ordering materials or preparing for a study, call an Ascension Press Study Consultant at 1-800-376-0520.

We welcome your feedback. Please contact us at AscensionPress.com or by mail at Ascension Press, P.O. Box 1990, West Chester, PA 19380.

Student workbook content begins on the next page.

A Letter from Fr. Mark Toups

Welcome to *Oremus*!* Over the next eight weeks, you are going to be inspired to deepen your prayer life while learning how to open yourself to God and receive everything he wants for you in prayer. As Catholics, we have a deep spiritual heritage in classic forms of prayer, including meditation, contemplation, and the spiritual senses. These rich forms of Christian prayer allow us to "dive deep" into the oceans of God's merciful love.

In her autobiography, St. Thérése of Lisieux describes prayer in this way: "For me, prayer is a surge of the heart; it is a simple look turned toward heaven; it is a cry of recognition and of love, embracing both trial and joy"[4] (CCC 2558). If you're hungry for this "surge of the heart," this study is for *you*.

Would you like to hear God speak to you? When many Catholics hear the words "meditation" and "contemplative prayer," their eyes glaze over and their thoughts wander. Such practices, they think, are reserved to priests, monks, and nuns; lay people certainly cannot do such things. Yet God calls all Christians, regardless of their state in life, to grow in holiness; this type of prayer provides the means to a deepened relationship with the Lord. However, all of us—including you—are invited to grow in an intimate relationship with God through the gift of prayer.

Oremus will provide you with the basics on both meditative and contemplative prayer, concentrating in a special way on a form of praying with the Bible known as *lectio divina,* as well as on "imaginative" prayer, a way of praying that allows the Holy Spirit to guide your spiritual senses. The principles of this study are drawn from the *Spiritual Exercises* of Saint Ignatius of Loyola.

About the *Oremus* program. There are eight sessions in the *Oremus* program. At each session, I will guide you through an easy-to-understand teaching on prayer. After each presentation, you will engage in a small-group discussion of the truths you just heard. You will also have a chance to talk about any challenges or developments you wish to share with the group from the previous week.

Here's the best part: In between sessions, you will be invited to pray using specific Scripture passages in your workbook. I'll give you a Scripture passage every day for the eight weeks. It's like making an eight-week retreat in the midst of your busy life! You will also be invited to keep track of your thoughts and progress through short journal entries that you will be making in your workbook. These weeks are designed to help guide you step-by-step to draw close to God and to listen for his voice speaking to you.

I'm looking forward to walking with you. See you soon at *Oremus!*

In Christ,

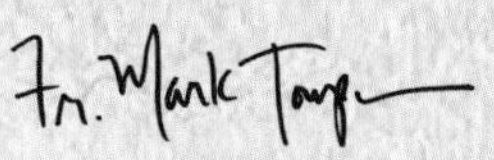

Fr. Mark Toups

**Oremus* \ō-'rā-müs\ is a Latin word meaning "Let us pray."

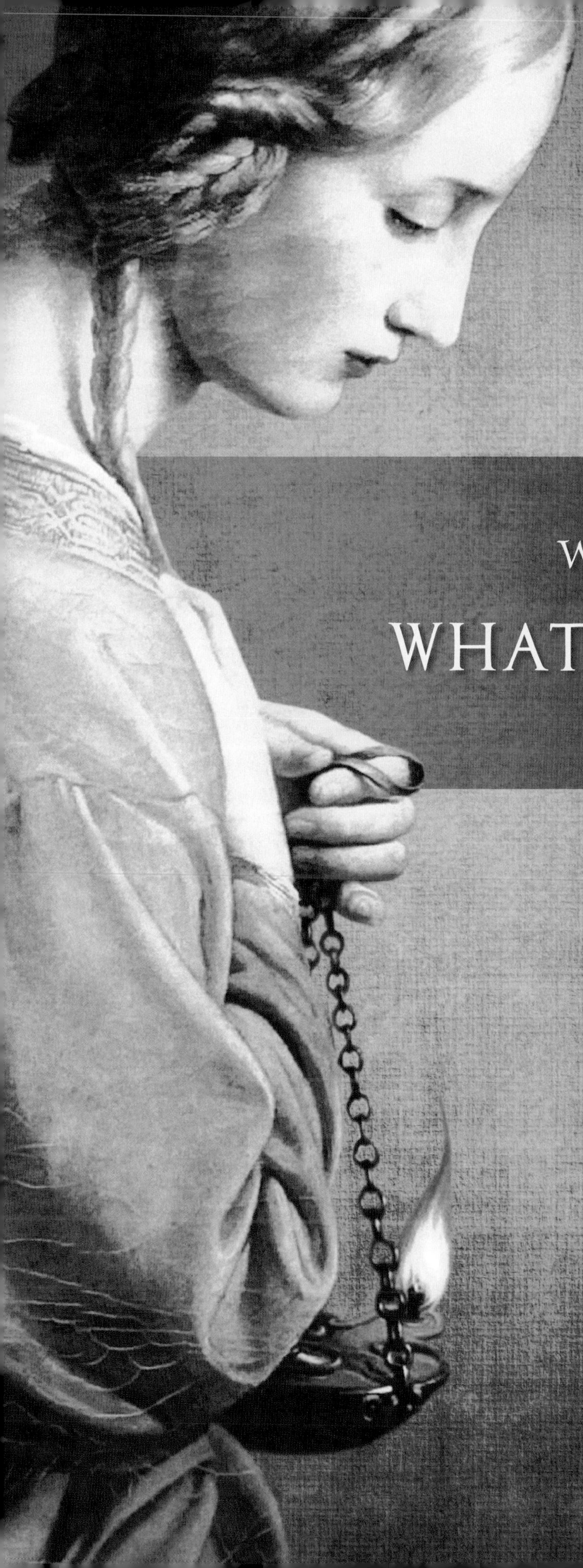

Week One:

What Is Prayer?

What Is Prayer?
SESSION OUTLINE

1. "*Man is in search of God.* In the act of creation, God calls every being from nothingness into existence. ... Even after losing through his sin his likeness to God, man remains an image of his Creator, and retains the desire for the one who calls him into existence. All religions bear witness to men's essential search for God." –CCC 2566[1]

2. "Human life without prayer, which opens our existence to the mystery God, lacks sense and direction." –Pope Benedict XVI[2]

3. "Many Christians are aware of the necessity and the beauty of contemplative prayer and have a sincere yearning for it. Yet, apart from tentative efforts soon abandoned, few remain faithful to this mode of prayer, and even fewer are really convinced and satisfied by their own practice of it. ... We would like to pray, but we cannot manage it. ... Our time of prayer passes, leaving us distracted, and since it does not seem to yield any tangible fruit, we are not loath to give up. From time to time we take up a book of 'meditations,' which presents us, ready-made, with the contemplation we ought to produce for ourselves. ... Often ... fearfulness ... robs us of the confidence to take steps on our own." –Hans Urs von Balthazar[3]

4. "He was praying in a certain place, and when he ceased, one of his disciples said to him, 'Lord, teach us to pray, as John taught his disciples.'" –Luke 11:1

5. "It is in fact in Jesus that man becomes able to approach God in the depth and intimacy of the relationship of fatherhood and sonship. Together with the first disciples, let us now turn with humble trust to the Teacher and ask him: 'Lord, teach us to pray.'" –Pope Benedict XVI[4]

6. “God calls man first. Man may forget his Creator or hide far from his face; he may run after idols or accuse the deity of having abandoned him; yet the living and true God tirelessly calls each person to that mysterious encounter known as prayer. In prayer ... God’s initiative of love always comes first; our own first step is always a response.” –CCC 2567

7. “It was not you who chose me but I who chose you.” –John 15:16, NAB

8. “A step or two before the place where I am to contemplate or meditate, I will stand for the space of an Our Father and, with my consciousness raised on high, consider how the Lord my God looks upon me. Then I will make an act of reverence or humility.” –St. Ignatius of Loyola[5]

9. “*We have come to believe in God’s love*: in these words the Christian can express the fundamental decision of his life. Being Christian is not the result of an ethical choice or a lofty idea, but the encounter with an event, a person, which gives life a new horizon and a decisive direction.” –Pope Benedict XVI[6]

10. “We receive the first lesson from the Lord by his example. The Gospels describe Jesus to us in intimate and constant conversation with the Father: it is a profound communion of the One who came into the world not to do his will but that of the Father who sent him for the salvation of man.” –Pope Benedict XVI[7]

11. “Yet only in God who reveals himself does man’s seeking find complete fulfillment. The prayer that is openness and elevation of the heart to God, thus becomes a personal relationship with him. And even if man forgets his Creator, the living, true God does not cease to call man first to the mysterious encounter of prayer.” –Pope Benedict XVI[8]

12. “For I know well the plans I have in mind for you, says the Lord, plans for your welfare, not for woe! plans to give you a future full of hope. When you call me, when you go to pray to me, I will listen to you. When you look for me, you will find me. Yes, when you seek me with all your heart, you will find me with you, says the Lord.” –Jeremiah 29:11-14, NAB

Discussion

QUESTION #1

What challenges do you face in your prayer life? Explain.

QUESTION #2

Describe your experience of prayer before hearing this week's teaching.

QUESTION #3

What stayed with you the most from the teaching this week?

QUESTION #4

What do you desire most from God as you begin this eight-week study?

QUESTION #5

What do you desire most from God during your prayer time?

Day 1
WEEK #1

FOR YOUR PRAYER

JEREMIAH 29:11-14

Read the passage once to become familiar with the text.
Slowly read the passage a second time.
Very, very slowly read the passage a third time.
Pay attention to which word, words, or phrases captures your attention or tugs at your heart.
Talk to God about what is on your heart … and listen.

JOURNAL

The "strongest" thought or feeling during my prayer was …

My heart "rested" when …

I sense the Lord was telling me …

I ended the prayer wanting …

Day 2
WEEK #1

FOR YOUR PRAYER

JOHN 15:1-17

Read the passage once to become familiar with the text.
Slowly read the passage a second time.
Very, very slowly read the passage a third time.
Pay attention to which word, words, or phrases captures your attention or tugs at your heart.
Talk to God about what is on your heart ... and listen.

JOURNAL

The "strongest" thought or feeling during my prayer was ...

My heart "rested" when ...

I sense the Lord was telling me ...

I ended the prayer wanting ...

Day 3
WEEK #1

FOR YOUR PRAYER

PSALMS 139:1-18

Read the passage once to become familiar with the text.

Slowly read the passage a second time.

Very, very slowly read the passage a third time.

Pay attention to which word, words, or phrases captures your attention or tugs at your heart.

Talk to God about what is on your heart … and listen.

JOURNAL

The "strongest" thought or feeling during my prayer was …

My heart "rested" when …

I sense the Lord was telling me …

I ended the prayer wanting …

Day 4
WEEK #1

FOR YOUR PRAYER

ROMANS 8:22-27

Read the passage once to become familiar with the text.

Slowly read the passage a second time.

Very, very slowly read the passage a third time.

Pay attention to which word, words, or phrases captures your attention or tugs at your heart.

Talk to God about what is on your heart ... and listen.

JOURNAL

The "strongest" thought or feeling during my prayer was ...

My heart "rested" when ...

I sense the Lord was telling me ...

I ended the prayer wanting ...

Day 5
WEEK #1

FOR YOUR PRAYER

ROMANS 8:31-39

Read the passage once to become familiar with the text.
Slowly read the passage a second time.
Very, very slowly read the passage a third time.
Pay attention to which word, words, or phrases captures your attention or tugs at your heart.
Talk to God about what is on your heart ... and listen.

JOURNAL

The "strongest" thought or feeling during my prayer was ...

My heart "rested" when ...

I sense the Lord was telling me ...

I ended the prayer wanting ...

Day 6

WEEK #1

FOR YOUR PRAYER

PSALM 63

Read the passage once to become familiar with the text.
Slowly read the passage a second time.
Very, very slowly read the passage a third time.
Pay attention to which word, words, or phrases captures your attention or tugs at your heart.
Talk to God about what is on your heart ... and listen.

JOURNAL

The "strongest" thought or feeling during my prayer was ...

My heart "rested" when ...

I sense the Lord was telling me ...

I ended the prayer wanting ...

Day 7

WEEK #1

FOR YOUR PRAYER

Return to the Scripture passage that spoke to you the most this week.

Read the passage once to become familiar with the text.

Slowly read the passage a second time.

Very, very slowly read the passage a third time.

Pay attention to which word, words, or phrases captures your attention or tugs at your heart.

Talk to God about what is on your heart ... and listen.

JOURNAL

The "strongest" thought or feeling during my prayer was ...

My heart "rested" when ...

I sense the Lord was telling me ...

I ended the prayer wanting ...

Week Two:

BEFORE YOU PRAY

Before You Pray
SESSION OUTLINE

Step One – Find the right time.

1. "Each one of us needs time and space for recollection, meditation, and calmness. ... Thanks be to God that this is so! In fact, this need tells us that we are not made for work alone, but also to think, to reflect or even simply to follow with our minds and our hearts a tale, a story in which to immerse ourselves, in a certain sense 'to lose ourselves' to find ourselves subsequently enriched." –Pope Benedict XVI[1]

2. "Making time for God regularly is a fundamental element for spiritual growth; it will be the Lord himself who gives us the taste for his mysteries, his words, his presence and action, for feeling how beautiful it is when God speaks with us; he will enable us to understand more deeply what he expects of me." –Pope Benedict XVI[2]

3. A few important questions about you:
   - When are you most receptive?
   - When are you most uninterrupted?
   - What time is most consistently open?

4. A few important questions about your commitments to other people:
   - What commitments have you made to your spouse?
   - What commitments have you made to your family?
   - What commitments have you made to others, such as to your job or school?

Consider: *Might any of these commitments need to be sacrificed or re-prioritized in order to meet your commitments to God?*

5. There's a difference between recreation and re-creation:
   - Start slow
   - Be realistic
   - Be consistent
   - Grow gradually

Step Two – Select a Scripture passage ahead of time.

6. "Through his Word, God speaks to man." –CCC 2700

7. How do you find a Scripture passage?
   - Readings for daily Mass
   - Readings for the upcoming Sunday
   - Slowly read through the Gospels: Mark, Matthew, Luke, John
   - Slowly read through the Psalms

Step Three – Pay attention to your desires.

8. "Saint Augustine, in a homily on the *First Letter of John*, describes very beautifully the intimate relationship between prayer and hope. He defines prayer as an exercise of desire." –Pope Benedict XVI[3]

9. "And if the object of one's desire is a relationship with God, his blessing and love, then the struggle cannot fail but ends in that self-giving to God, in recognition of one's own weakness, which is overcome only by giving oneself over into God's merciful hands." –Pope Benedict XVI[4]

10. "We would not be able to pray were the desire for God, for being children of God, not engraved in the depths of our heart." –Pope Benedict XVI[5]

11. "I will ask my Lord for what I want and desire." –St. Ignatius of Loyola[6]

Discussion

QUESTION #1

How would you describe your experience of prayer this past week?

QUESTION #2

What did you find most interesting from this week's teaching?

QUESTION #3

What is the best time for you to pray?
What challenges do you face with being consistent with this time?

QUESTION #4

How would you describe your overall experience of praying with Scripture?
Is it easy? Is it difficult? Explain.

QUESTION #5

How important are your desires to your prayer? Do you share them with God?
Do you tend to ignore them? Do you feel they are important?

Day 1

WEEK #2

FOR YOUR PRAYER

MATTHEW 11:28-30

Read the passage once to become familiar with the text.
Slowly read the passage a second time.
Very, very slowly read the passage a third time.
Pay attention to which word, words, or phrases captures your attention or tugs at your heart.
Talk to God about what is on your heart … and listen.

JOURNAL

The "strongest" thought or feeling during my prayer was …

My heart "rested" when …

I sense the Lord was telling me …

I ended the prayer wanting …

Day 2
WEEK #2

FOR YOUR PRAYER

ISAIAH 55

Read the passage once to become familiar with the text.

Slowly read the passage a second time.

Very, very slowly read the passage a third time.

Pay attention to which word, words, or phrases captures your attention or tugs at your heart.

Talk to God about what is on your heart … and listen.

JOURNAL

The "strongest" thought or feeling during my prayer was …

My heart "rested" when …

I sense the Lord was telling me …

I ended the prayer wanting …

DAY 3

WEEK #2

FOR YOUR PRAYER

ISAIAH 43:1-7

Read the passage once to become familiar with the text.
Slowly read the passage a second time.
Very, very slowly read the passage a third time.
Pay attention to which word, words, or phrases captures your attention or tugs at your heart.
Talk to God about what is on your heart … and listen.

JOURNAL

The "strongest" thought or feeling during my prayer was …

My heart "rested" when …

I sense the Lord was telling me …

I ended the prayer wanting …

Day 4

WEEK #2

FOR YOUR PRAYER

MARK 10:46-52

Read the passage once to become familiar with the text.
Slowly read the passage a second time.
Very, very slowly read the passage a third time.
Pay attention to which word, words, or phrases captures your attention or tugs at your heart.
Talk to God about what is on your heart … and listen.

JOURNAL

The "strongest" thought or feeling during my prayer was …

My heart "rested" when …

I sense the Lord was telling me …

I ended the prayer wanting …

DAY 5

WEEK #2

FOR YOUR PRAYER

ISAIAH 26:8-13

Read the passage once to become familiar with the text.
Slowly read the passage a second time.
Very, very slowly read the passage a third time.
Pay attention to which word, words, or phrases captures your attention or tugs at your heart.
Talk to God about what is on your heart … and listen.

JOURNAL

The "strongest" thought or feeling during my prayer was …

My heart "rested" when …

I sense the Lord was telling me …

I ended the prayer wanting …

DAY 6
WEEK #2

FOR YOUR PRAYER

MATTHEW 18:12-14

Read the passage once to become familiar with the text.
Slowly read the passage a second time.
Very, very slowly read the passage a third time.
Pay attention to which word, words, or phrases captures your attention or tugs at your heart.
Talk to God about what is on your heart ... and listen.

JOURNAL

The "strongest" thought or feeling during my prayer was ...

My heart "rested" when ...

I sense the Lord was telling me ...

I ended the prayer wanting ...

DAY 7

WEEK #2

FOR YOUR PRAYER

Return to the Scripture passage that spoke to you the most this week.
Read the passage once to become familiar with the text.
Slowly read the passage a second time.
Very, very slowly read the passage a third time.
Pay attention to which word, words, or phrases captures your attention or tugs at your heart.
Talk to God about what is on your heart ... and listen.

JOURNAL

The "strongest" thought or feeling during my prayer was ...

My heart "rested" when ...

I sense the Lord was telling me ...

I ended the prayer wanting ...

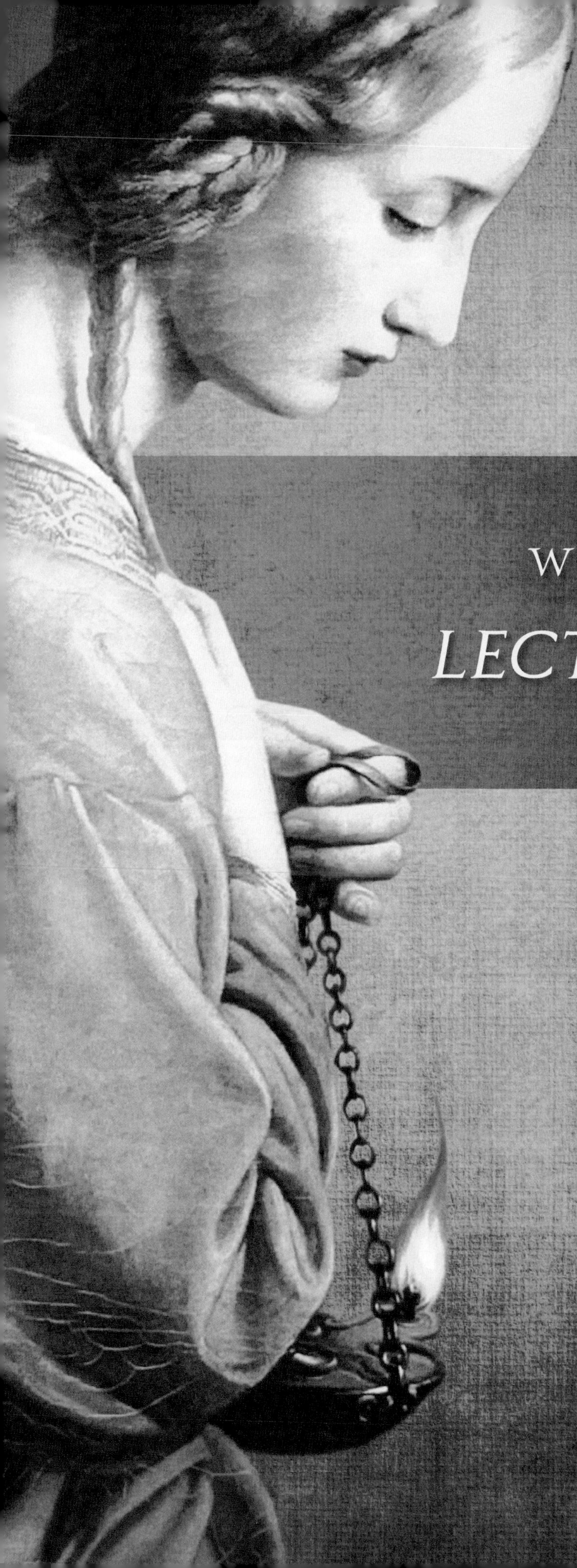

Week Three:

Lectio Divina

Lectio Divina

SESSION OUTLINE

"I would like in particular to recall and recommend the ancient tradition of *lectio divina:* the diligent reading of Sacred Scripture accompanied by prayer brings about that intimate dialogue in which the person reading hears God who is speaking, and in praying, responds to him with trusting openness of heart. If it is effectively promoted, this practice will bring to the Church—I am convinced of it—a new spiritual springtime." –Pope Benedict XVI[1]

Lectio Divina

Lectio divina (sometimes known simply as "*lectio*") is Latin for "divine reading."

Step One: *Lectio*

- Start with a passage from Scripture and become familiar with the text.

- Slowly read the passage a second time.

- Very, very slowly read the passage a third time.

- Pay attention to which word, words, or phrases rest in your heart.

Step Two: *Meditatio*

- Think about the significant text ... what is God saying to you?

- What are the implications of the text in your life?

- "To meditate on what we read helps us to make it our own by confronting it with ourselves. Here, another book is opened: the book of life. ... To the extent that we are humble and faithful, we discover in meditation the movements that stir the heart and we are able to discern them." –CCC 2706

Step Three: *Oratio*

- Talk to God ... talk with God ... about everything.

- "What is contemplative prayer? St. Teresa answers: 'Contemplative prayer *[oracion mental]* in my opinion is nothing else than a close sharing between friends. ... In this inner prayer we can still meditate, but our attention is fixed on the Lord himself." –CCC 2709[2]

Step Four: *Contemplatio*

- Rest in God's presence.

- "Contemplative prayer is also the pre-eminently intense time of prayer. In it the Father strengthens our inner being with power through his Spirit 'that Christ may dwell in [our] hearts through faith' and we may be 'grounded in love.'" –CCC 2714[3]

- "Where does prayer come from? Whether prayer is expressed in words or gestures, it is the whole man who prays. But in naming the source of prayer, Scripture speaks sometimes of the soul or the spirit, but most often of the heart (more than a thousand times). According to Scripture, it is the *heart* that prays. If our heart is far from God, the words of prayer are in vain." –CCC 2562

Discussion

QUESTION #1

Was there anything in the teaching this week that surprised you or caused you to rethink your desire to pray with the Scriptures?

QUESTION #2

Describe your experience of prayer this past week.
Do you feel as if things are getting "easier" as you pray?

QUESTION #3

Of the four steps of *lectio divina,* which do you think would be the easiest for you to enter into?
Which do you think would be the most difficult?

QUESTION #4

How you feel *lectio divina* can help you as you pray?

QUESTION #5

Have you made any strides in working through some of your challenges these past few weeks?
What challenges still exist?

DAY 1
WEEK #3

FOR YOUR PRAYER

LUKE 12:22-32

Practice the art of *lectio divina.*

JOURNAL

The "strongest" thought or feeling during my prayer was ...

My heart "rested" when ...

I sense the Lord was telling me ...

I ended the prayer wanting ...

Day 2
WEEK #3

FOR YOUR PRAYER

PSALM 27

Practice the art of *lectio divina.*

JOURNAL

The "strongest" thought or feeling during my prayer was …

My heart "rested" when …

I sense the Lord was telling me …

I ended the prayer wanting …

Day 3

WEEK #3

FOR YOUR PRAYER

PSALM 23

Practice the art of *lectio divina.*

JOURNAL

The "strongest" thought or feeling during my prayer was ...

My heart "rested" when ...

I sense the Lord was telling me ...

I ended the prayer wanting ...

DAY 4
WEEK #3

FOR YOUR PRAYER

JOHN 4:7-19

Practice the art of *lectio divina.*

JOURNAL

The "strongest" thought or feeling during my prayer was ...

My heart "rested" when ...

I sense the Lord was telling me ...

I ended the prayer wanting ...

DAY 5
WEEK #3

FOR YOUR PRAYER

WISDOM 11:21-26

Practice the art of *lectio divina.*

JOURNAL

The "strongest" thought or feeling during my prayer was ...

My heart "rested" when ...

I sense the Lord was telling me ...

I ended the prayer wanting ...

Day 6

WEEK #3

FOR YOUR PRAYER

DEUTERONOMY 7:6-8

Practice the art of *lectio divina.*

JOURNAL

The "strongest" thought or feeling during my prayer was ...

My heart "rested" when ...

I sense the Lord was telling me ...

I ended the prayer wanting ...

DAY 7

WEEK #3

FOR YOUR PRAYER

Return to the Scripture passage that spoke to you the most this week.
Practice the art of *lectio divina.*

JOURNAL

The "strongest" thought or feeling during my prayer was ...

My heart "rested" when ...

I sense the Lord was telling me ...

I ended the prayer wanting ...

Week Four:

Relational Prayer

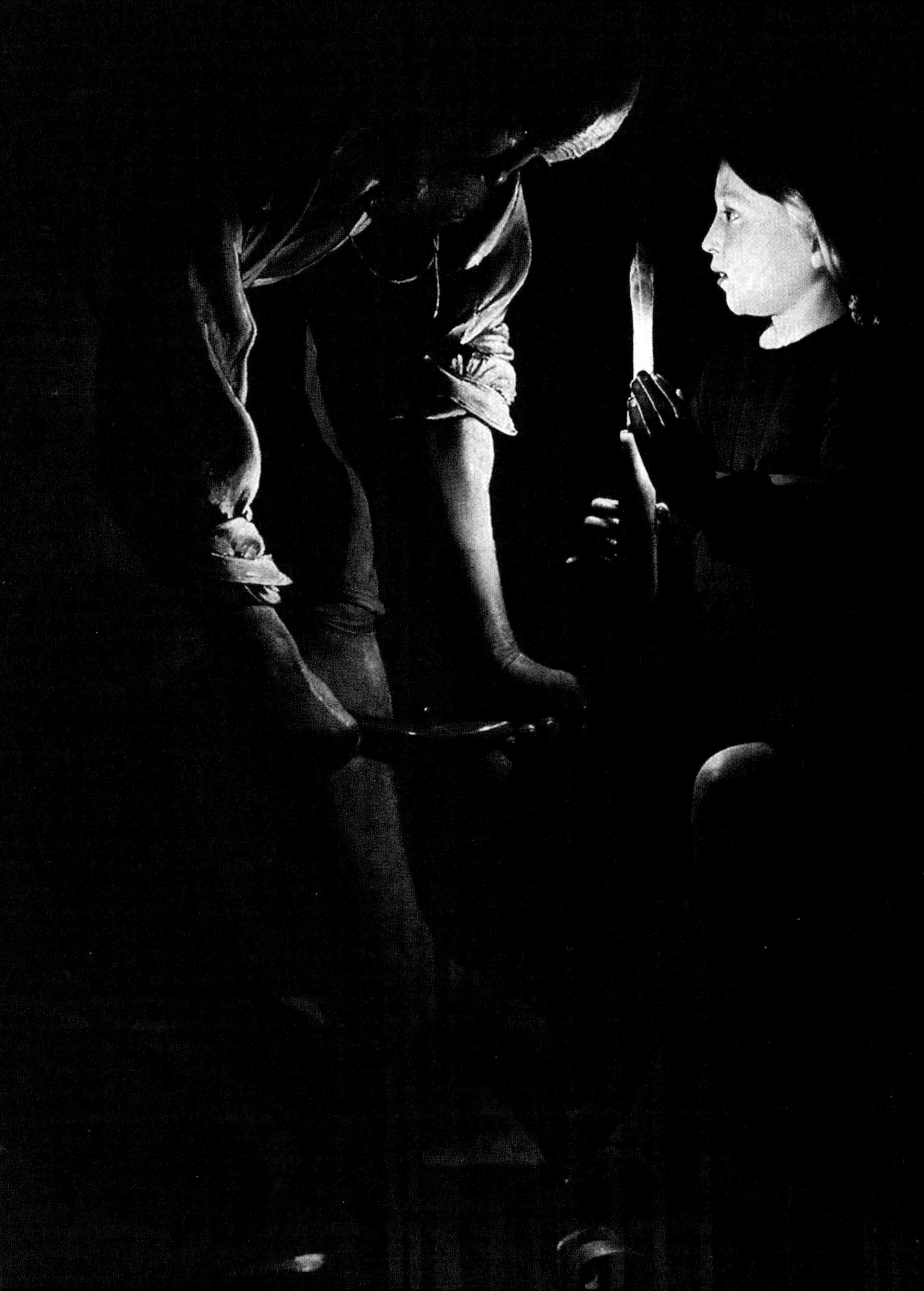

Relational Prayer
SESSION OUTLINE

1. The four steps to relational prayer—prayer in which God reaches out to us, and we respond to his loving approach—may be summed up by the acronym *A.R.R.R.* The four steps are:
   - Acknowledge
   - Relate
   - Receive
   - Respond

2. "Mary is the perfect *Orans* (pray-er), a figure of the Church." –CCC 2679

Step One: Acknowledge

3. "God calls man first. Man may forget his Creator or hide far from his face; he may run after idols or accuse the deity of having abandoned him; yet the living and true God tirelessly calls each person to that mysterious encounter known as prayer. In prayer … God's initiative of love always comes first; our own first step is always a response." –CCC 2567

Step Two: Relate

4. "Where does prayer come from? Whether prayer is expressed in words or gestures, it is the whole man who prays. But in naming the source of prayer, Scripture speaks sometimes of the soul or the spirit, but most often of the heart (more than a thousand times). According to Scripture, it is the heart that prays. If our heart is far from God, the words of prayer are in vain." –CCC 2562

5. "In learning how to speak to him, we learn to be a human being, to be ourselves." –Pope Benedict XVI[1]

6. Tips for "Relating" to God.

- Don't just think about God; talk to God.
- Be aware. Be honest. Nothing is "off limits."
- Remember Psalm 139:4 (RSV:CE). "Even before a word is on my tongue, behold, O LORD, you know it altogether."
- Pay attention to what you do not want to say.

Step Three: Receive

7. "Always expressed in every prayer ... is the truth of the human creature who on the one hand experiences weakness and impoverishment, who therefore addresses his supplication to Heaven, and on the other is endowed with an extraordinary dignity, so that, in preparing to receive the divine Revelation, finds himself able to enter into communion with God." –Pope Benedict XVI[2]

8. "God speaks in silence, but we must know how to listen." –Pope Benedict XVI[3]

9. Tips for "Receiving" from God.

- Listen. Listen with all your spiritual senses.
- Be patient. Don't be afraid of the silence.
- Could be a voice ... a song ... a memory ... an image ... a sensation in your body ... a Scripture passage.

Step Four: Respond

10. "The 'yes' of God is not halved, it is not somewhere between 'yes' and 'no,' but is a sound and simple 'yes.' And we respond to this 'yes' with our own 'yes,' with our 'amen,' and so we are sure of the 'yes' of God." –Pope Benedict XVI[4]

11. Tips for "Responding" to God.

- Respond to what you have received.
- Could be more conversation ... question ... laughter ... tears ... "yes."
- Together, the four steps of relational prayer (A.R.R.R.) are a vibrant dynamic, not a systematic checklist.

Discussion

QUESTION #1

How would you describe your experience in prayer this past week?

QUESTION #2

Was there anything in the teaching this week that really stands out to you?

QUESTION #3

We've said that the four steps of relational prayer are:
Acknowledge. Relate. Receive. Respond. (A.R.R.R.)
How could these four distinct steps or movements help you
to relate to God more deeply during prayer?

QUESTION #4

Which movement within A.R.R.R. is most helpful to you? Which movement is most challenging?

QUESTION #5

Are you experiencing any obstacles in your prayer?
If so, do you feel like you can be honest with God about those challenges?

Day 1
WEEK #4

FOR YOUR PRAYER

PSALM 91

Practice the art of *lectio divina.*

Consider how God is the author of all creation.

***Note:** *Please also read the prayer assignment for tomorrow so that you may adequately prepare.*

JOURNAL

The "strongest" thought or feeling during my prayer was ...

My heart "rested" when ...

I sense the Lord was telling me ...

I ended the prayer wanting ...

Day 2
WEEK #4

FOR YOUR PRAYER

Genesis 1

Watch the sunrise and pray with Genesis 1.

Consider how all of creation is a gift from God, and how all of creation blesses God.

***Note:** *Please also read the prayer assignment for tomorrow so that you may adequately prepare.*

JOURNAL

The "strongest" thought or feeling during my prayer was ...

My heart "rested" when ...

I sense the Lord was telling me ...

I ended the prayer wanting ...

DAY 3
WEEK #4

FOR YOUR PRAYER

DANIEL 3:35-68

(*"The Song of the Three Young Men"* in RSV-CE)

Watch the sunset and pray with Daniel 3:35-68.

Practice the art of *lectio divina*.

Consider how all of creation is a gift from God, and how all of creation blesses God.

JOURNAL

The "strongest" thought or feeling during my prayer was ...

My heart "rested" when ...

I sense the Lord was telling me ...

I ended the prayer wanting ...

DAY 4
WEEK #4

FOR YOUR PRAYER

DANIEL 3:35-68

Practice the art of *lectio divina.*

Consider how all of creation is a gift from God, and how all of creation blesses God.

JOURNAL

The "strongest" thought or feeling during my prayer was ...

My heart "rested" when ...

I sense the Lord was telling me ...

I ended the prayer wanting ...

Day 5
WEEK #4

FOR YOUR PRAYER

PHILIPPIANS 4:11-13

Practice the art of *lectio divina.*

Ask God for the grace to want him more than you want anything else in this life.

JOURNAL

The "strongest" thought or feeling during my prayer was ...

My heart "rested" when ...

I sense the Lord was telling me ...

I ended the prayer wanting ...

Day 6
WEEK #4

FOR YOUR PRAYER

PHILIPPIANS 4:11-13

Pray once more with Philippians 4:11-13.

Ask God again for the grace to want him more than you want anything else in this life.

JOURNAL

The "strongest" thought or feeling during my prayer was ...

My heart "rested" when ...

I sense the Lord was telling me ...

I ended the prayer wanting ...

DAY 7
WEEK #4

FOR YOUR PRAYER

Return to the Scripture passage that spoke to you the most this week.
Practice the art of *lectio divina.*
Thank the Lord for all that he has done for you.

JOURNAL

The "strongest" thought or feeling during my prayer was ...

My heart "rested" when ...

I sense the Lord was telling me ...

I ended the prayer wanting ...

Week Five:

Spiritual Senses

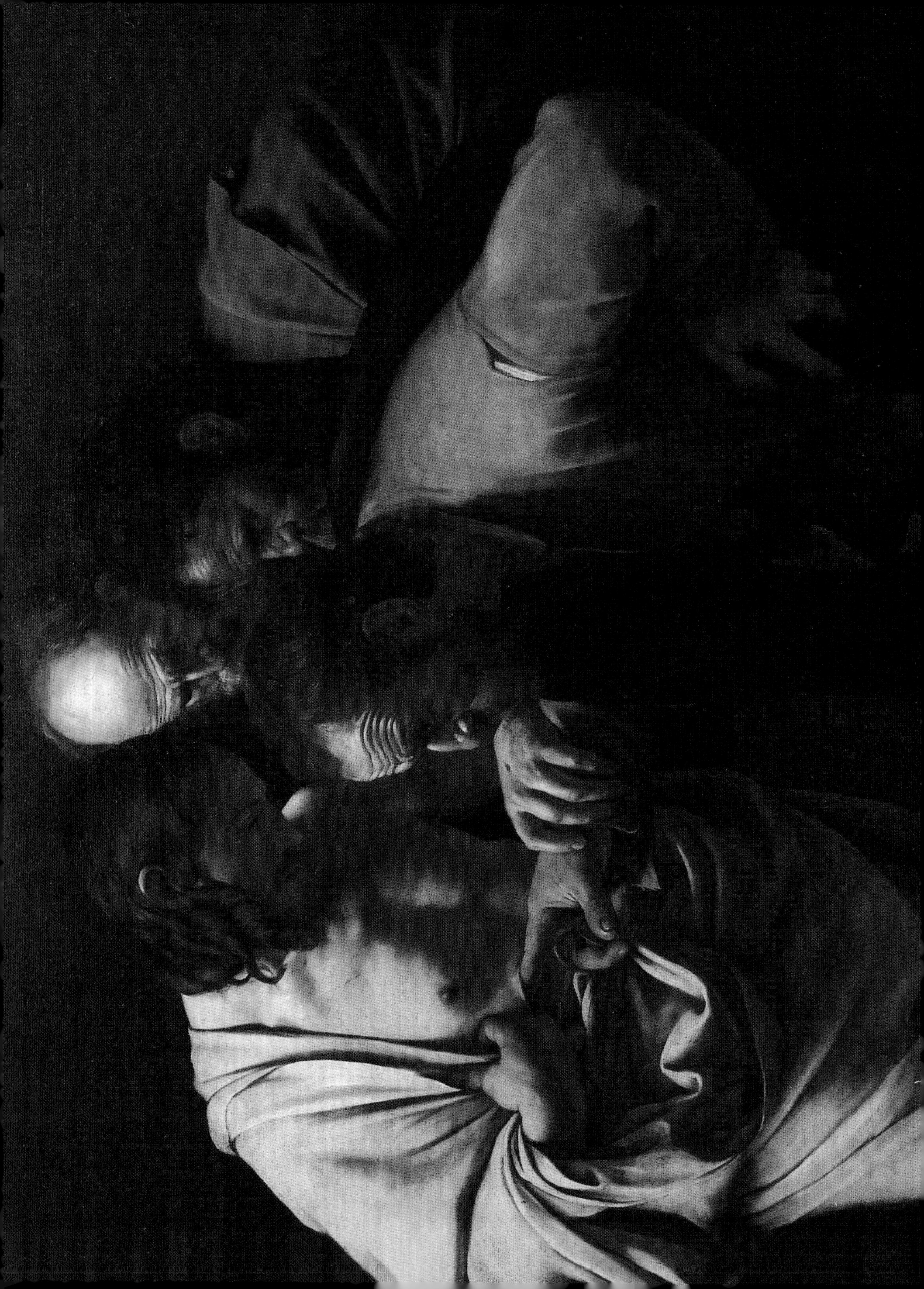

Spiritual Senses
SESSION OUTLINE

1. "Meditation engages thought, imagination, emotion, and desire. ... Christian prayer tries above all to meditate on the mysteries of Christ, as in *lectio divina* or the rosary. This form of prayerful reflection is of great value, but Christian prayer should go further: to the knowledge of the love of the Lord Jesus, to union with him." –CCC 2708

2. "Meditation is a prayerful quest engaging thought, imagination, emotion, and desire. Its goal is to make our own in faith the subject considered, by confronting it with the reality of our own life." –CCC 2723

3. Imaginative prayer requires the use of our spiritual senses. Our spiritual senses, used in imaginative prayer, are:
   - Interior sight
   - Interior listening
   - Interior smell
   - Interior feeling
   - Interior tasting

4. "In this manner of praying, Saint Ignatius tells us, we imaginatively see the persons in the Bible passage, we hear the words they speak, and we observe the actions they accomplish in the event." –Fr. Tim Gallagher, O.M.V.[1]

Discussion

QUESTION #1

Describe your experience of prayer this past week.

QUESTION #2

In what ways is your experience of prayer changing? In what ways is it still the same?

QUESTION #3

How can using your spiritual senses and your imagination help you as you pray? What challenges, if any, would you anticipate with imaginative prayer?

QUESTION #4

What stirs in your heart as you gaze at the Caravaggio painting?

QUESTION #5

If you could be a part of a scene in Jesus' life, which scene would you like to enter? Explain.

DAY 1
WEEK #5

FOR YOUR PRAYER

JOHN 20:19-29

Practice the art of imaginative prayer.

Be *in* the scene.

You are Thomas ... touch Jesus' wounds.

Let Jesus touch your heart ... and listen.

JOURNAL

The "strongest" thought or feeling during my prayer was ...

My heart "rested" when ...

I sense the Lord was telling me ...

I ended the prayer wanting ...

Day 2
WEEK #5

FOR YOUR PRAYER

JOHN 3:22-30

Practice the art of imaginative prayer.
Be *in* the scene.
Listen to verse 30 … What is John saying to *you*?
Talk to God about what is on your heart … and listen.

JOURNAL

The "strongest" thought or feeling during my prayer was …

My heart "rested" when …

I sense the Lord was telling me …

I ended the prayer wanting …

DAY 3

WEEK #5

FOR YOUR PRAYER

LUKE 17:11-19

Practice the art of imaginative prayer.

Be *in* the scene.

Listen to verses 17-18 … Where have *you* been ungrateful?

Talk to God about what is on your heart … and listen.

JOURNAL

The "strongest" thought or feeling during my prayer was …

My heart "rested" when …

I sense the Lord was telling me …

I ended the prayer wanting …

DAY 4
WEEK #5

FOR YOUR PRAYER

MATTHEW 14:22-33

Practice the art of imaginative prayer.

Be *in* the scene.

You are Peter ... *Why* do you take your eyes off of Jesus?

Talk to God about what is on your heart ... and listen.

JOURNAL

The "strongest" thought or feeling during my prayer was ...

My heart "rested" when ...

I sense the Lord was telling me ...

I ended the prayer wanting ...

Day 5

WEEK #5

FOR YOUR PRAYER

MATTHEW 19:16-26

Practice the art of imaginative prayer.

Be *in* the scene.

You are the rich young man … Why do you walk away?

Talk to God about what is on your heart … and listen.

JOURNAL

The "strongest" thought or feeling during my prayer was …

My heart "rested" when …

I sense the Lord was telling me …

I ended the prayer wanting …

Day 6
WEEK #5

FOR YOUR PRAYER

JOHN 13:31-38

Practice the art of imaginative prayer.
Be *in* the scene.
You are Peter ... What stirs in your heart as Jesus makes his prediction?
Talk to God about what is on your heart ... and listen.

JOURNAL

The "strongest" thought or feeling during my prayer was ...

My heart "rested" when ...

I sense the Lord was telling me ...

I ended the prayer wanting ...

Day 7

WEEK #5

FOR YOUR PRAYER

JOHN 18:15-18, 25-27

Practice the art of imaginative prayer.

Be *in* the scene.

You are Peter ... What stirs in your heart as *you* deny Jesus?

Talk to God about what is on your heart ... and listen.

JOURNAL

The "strongest" thought or feeling during my prayer was ...

My heart "rested" when ...

I sense the Lord was telling me ...

I ended the prayer wanting ...

Week Six:

Discernment in Prayer

Discernment In Prayer
SESSION OUTLINE

1. How do I know it is God who is speaking to me?

2. "In persons who are going from mortal sin to mortal sin, the enemy is ordinarily accustomed to propose apparent pleasures to them, leading them to imagine sensual delights and pleasures in order to hold them more and make them grow in their vices and sins. In these persons the good spirit uses a contrary method, stinging and biting their consciences through their rational power of moral judgment." –St. Ignatius of Loyola[1]

3. Going from mortal sin to mortal sin:
   - Temptation: propose apparent pleasures
   - Temptation: imagine sensual delights and pleasures
   - Temptation: hold them more, make them grow in vices and sins
   - God: stinging and biting the conscience

4. "In persons who are going on intensely purifying their sins and rising from good to better in the service of God our Lord, the method is contrary to that in the first rule. For then it is proper to the evil spirit to bite, sadden, and place obstacles, disquieting with false reasons, so that the person may not go forward. And it is proper of the good spirit to give courage and strength, consolations, tears, inspirations, and quiet, easing and taking away all obstacles, so that the person may go forward in doing good." –St. Ignatius of Loyola[2]

5. Going on intensely purifying their sins and rising from good to better:

- **Temptation:**
  - bite
  - sadden
  - place obstacles
  - disquieting with false reasons
  - so that the person may not go forward
- **God:**
  - give courage and strength
  - consolations
  - tears
  - inspirations
  - quiet
  - easing and taking away all obstacles
  - so that the person may go forward in doing good

6. "We should give much attention to the course of the thoughts; and if the beginning, middle and end is all good, inclined to all good, it is a sign of the good angel; but if in the course of the thoughts that he brings, it ends in something bad, or distractive, or less good than the soul had proposed to do before, or if it weakens it, or disquiets, or troubles the soul, taking away the peace, tranquility and quiet, which it had before, it is a clear sign that it proceeds from the bad spirit, the enemy of our profit and eternal salvation." –St. Ignatius of Loyola[3]

7. "In those who proceed from good to better, the good angel touches such a soul sweetly, lightly and gently, as a drop of water that enters a sponge; and the bad touches it sharply and with noise and disquiet, as when the drop of water falls on a stone; and in those who proceed from bad to worse the above-said spirits touch in a contrary way; the cause of which is that the disposition of the soul is contrary or similar to the said angels; for when it is contrary, they enter with clamor and sensible disturbances, perceptibly; and when it is similar, they enter with silence, as in their own house through an open door." –St. Ignatius of Loyola[4]

Discussion

QUESTION #1

Did you feel the "shift" in the Scripture passages this past week?
How would you describe your experience of prayer this past week?

QUESTION #2

Did you try using your spiritual senses and imagination in your prayer?
How would you describe your experience?

QUESTION #3

Was there anything in the teaching this week that surprised you or made you think differently?

QUESTION #4

Is it difficult for you to discern "what" you hear in prayer?

QUESTION #5

Notice how tenderly the Good Samaritan is gently cleaning in the Jacopo Bassano painting.
What stirs within you as you gaze at the painting?

Day 1

WEEK #6

FOR YOUR PRAYER

PSALM 51

Practice the art of *lectio divina.*

Be *specific* ... How have you sinned *specifically?*

Talk to God about what is on your heart ... and listen.

After you are finished with your prayer, rewrite Psalm 51 in your own words on the following page.

JOURNAL

The "strongest" thought or feeling during my prayer was ...

My heart "rested" when ...

I sense the Lord was telling me ...

I ended the prayer wanting ...

Rewrite Psalm 51 in your own words.

DAY 2
WEEK #6

FOR YOUR PRAYER

PSALM 6

Practice the art of *lectio divina.*

Ask God to reveal your sins to you.

Talk to God about what is on your heart ... and listen.

JOURNAL

The "strongest" thought or feeling during my prayer was ...

My heart "rested" when ...

I sense the Lord was telling me ...

I ended the prayer wanting ...

Day 3
WEEK #6

FOR YOUR PRAYER

LUKE 15:11-16

Practice the art of imaginative prayer.
In the scene, *you* are the son who leaves.
Why do you leave? What's your *pattern* of sin?
Talk to God about what is on your heart … and listen.

JOURNAL

The "strongest" thought or feeling during my prayer was …

My heart "rested" when …

I sense the Lord was telling me …

I ended the prayer wanting …

Day 4

WEEK #6

FOR YOUR PRAYER

Romans 7:11-19

Practice the art of *lectio divina.*

Ask God to reveal the root of your sin.

Talk to God about what is on your heart … and listen.

After you are finished with your prayer, rewrite Romans 7:11-19 in your own words on the following page.

JOURNAL

The "strongest" thought or feeling during my prayer was …

My heart "rested" when …

I sense the Lord was telling me …

I ended the prayer wanting …

Rewrite Romans 7:11-19 in your own words.

DAY 5

WEEK #6

FOR YOUR PRAYER

JOHN 8:1-11

Practice the art of imaginative prayer.
In the scene, *you* are the woman caught in adultery.
What is it like for you to raise your head and look at Jesus, *eye to eye*?
Talk to God about what is on your heart.

JOURNAL

The "strongest" thought or feeling during my prayer was ...

My heart "rested" when ...

I sense the Lord was telling me ...

I ended the prayer wanting ...

Day 6
WEEK #6

FOR YOUR PRAYER

Psalm 51

Again, pray with this psalm.
Practice the art of *lectio divina.*
Ask God to reveal your sins to you.
Talk to God about what is on your heart … and listen.

JOURNAL

The "strongest" thought or feeling during my prayer was …

____

____

____

____

My heart "rested" when …

____

____

____

____

I sense the Lord was telling me …

____

____

____

____

I ended the prayer wanting …

____

____

____

____

Day 7
WEEK #6

FOR YOUR PRAYER

PSALM 51

Again, pray with Psalm 51.
Practice the art of *lectio divina.*
Ask God to reveal your sins to you.
Talk to God about what is on your heart … and listen.

JOURNAL

The "strongest" thought or feeling during my prayer was …

My heart "rested" when …

I sense the Lord was telling me …

I ended the prayer wanting …

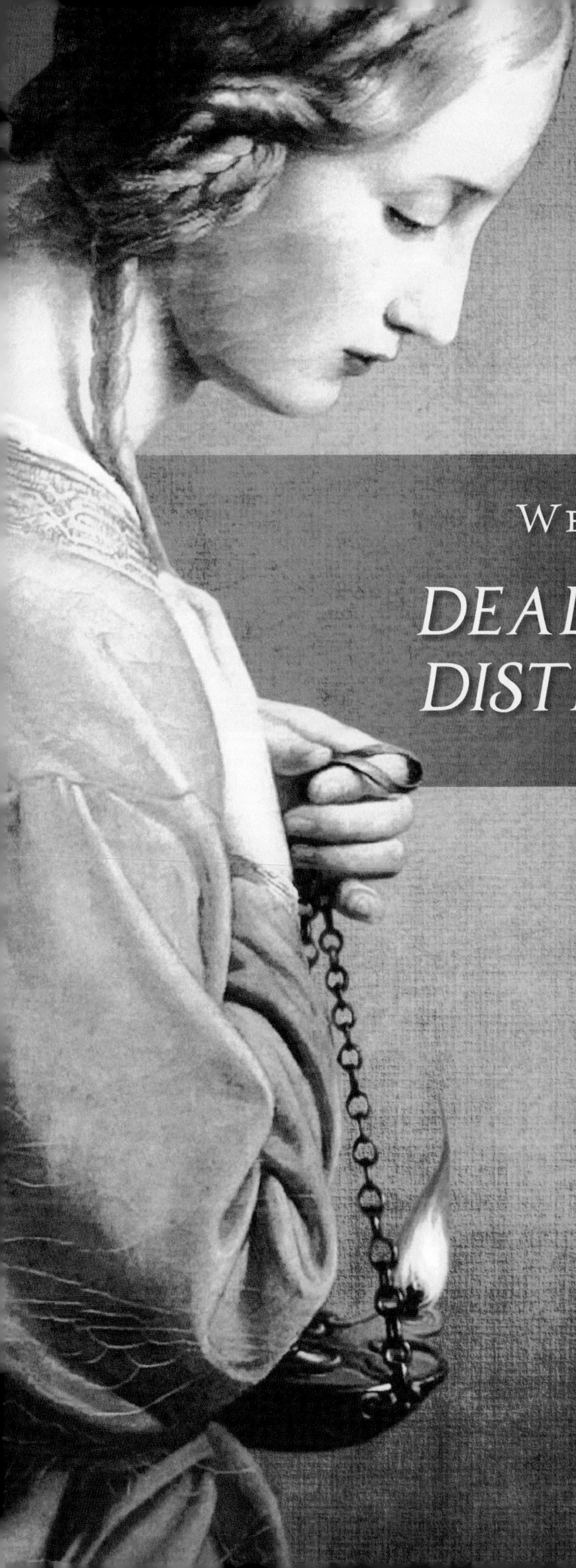

Week Seven:
Dealing with Distractions

Dealing With Distractions
SESSION OUTLINE

1. "In the battle of prayer, we must face in ourselves and around us *erroneous notions of prayer.* Some people view prayer as a simple psychological activity, others as an effort of concentration to reach a mental void. Still others reduce prayer to ritual words and postures. ... Those who seek God by prayer are quickly discouraged because they do not know that prayer comes also from the Holy Spirit and not from themselves alone." –CCC 2726

2. "We must also face the fact that certain attitudes deriving from the mentality of 'this present world' can penetrate our lives if we are not vigilant. ... Others overly prize production and profit; thus prayer, being unproductive, is useless. ... Finally, some see prayer as a flight from the world in reaction against activism; but in fact, Christian prayer is neither an escape from reality nor a divorce from life." –CCC 2727

3. "Prayer is both a gift of grace and a determined response on our part. It always presupposes effort. The great figures of prayer of the Old Covenant before Christ, as well as the Mother of God, the saints, and he himself, all teach us this: prayer is a battle. Against whom? Against ourselves and against the wiles of the tempter who does all he can to turn man away from prayer, away from union with God." –CCC 2725

4. "Finally, our battle has to confront what we experience as *failure in prayer*: discouragement during periods of dryness ... disappointment over not being heard according to our own will; wounded pride, stiffened by the indignity that is ours as sinners; our resistance to the idea that prayer is a free and unmerited gift; and so forth. The conclusion is always the same: what good does it do to pray? To overcome these obstacles, we must battle to gain humility, trust, and perseverance." –CCC 2728

5. "The enemy acts like a [spoiled child] in being weak when faced with strength and strong when faced with weakness. For, as it is proper to a [child], when he is fighting with [a firm adult], to lose heart and to flee when the [adult] confronts him firmly, and, on the contrary, if the [adult] begins to flee, losing heart, the anger, vengeance and ferocity of the [child] grow greatly and know no bounds, in the same way, it is proper to the enemy to weaken and lose heart, fleeing and ceasing his temptations when the person who is exercising himself in spiritual things confronts the temptations of the enemy firmly, doing what is diametrically opposed to them; and, on the contrary, if the person who is exercising himself begins to be afraid and lose heart in suffering the temptations, there is no beast so fierce on the face of the earth as the enemy of human nature in following out his damnable intention with such growing malice." –St. Ignatius of Loyola[1]

Discussion

QUESTION #1

Describe your experience of prayer this past week.

QUESTION #2

How would describe our culture's opinion of sin?
How would describe your opinion of sin?

QUESTION #3

Gaze at Rembrandt's painting of the Prodigal Son. What stirs within you?

QUESTION #4

What is your experience of distractions?
What are some of the more common distractions you experience?
How do you generally deal with distractions?

QUESTION #5

What interested you most during this week's teaching?

DAY 1

WEEK #7

FOR YOUR PRAYER

LUKE 15:11-24

Practice the art of imaginative prayer.

In the scene, *you* are the prodigal son.

Focus on the Father's eyes in verse 20.

Notice the Father's compassion.

What is the Father saying to you in his eyes?

JOURNAL

The "strongest" thought or feeling during my prayer was ...

My heart "rested" when ...

I sense the Lord was telling me ...

I ended the prayer wanting ...

Day 2
WEEK #7

FOR YOUR PRAYER

LUKE 7:36-50

Practice the art of imaginative prayer.
In the scene, you are at Jesus' feet ... focus on verse 48.
Look *at* Jesus. What is Jesus saying *to you* in his eyes?
Talk to God about what is on your heart ... and listen.

JOURNAL

The "strongest" thought or feeling during my prayer was ...

My heart "rested" when ...

I sense the Lord was telling me ...

I ended the prayer wanting ...

DAY 3
WEEK #7

FOR YOUR PRAYER

EZEKIEL 36:23-29

Practice the art of *lectio divina.*

Talk to God about what is on your heart ... and listen.

Make a commitment to go to a Catholic priest to receive the sacrament of reconciliation this week.*

JOURNAL

The "strongest" thought or feeling during my prayer was ...

My heart "rested" when ...

I sense the Lord was telling me ...

I ended the prayer wanting ...

*Most parishes offer confessions on Saturdays, but if you have scheduling difficulties many parishes are willing to schedule a specific time for you if you call in advance.

Day 4

WEEK #7

FOR YOUR PRAYER

1 PETER 2:21-25

Pray with 1 Peter 2:21-25.

Thank Jesus for his sacrifice, for the Church he founded, and for the sacrament of reconciliation.

JOURNAL

The "strongest" thought or feeling during my prayer was ...

My heart "rested" when ...

I sense the Lord was telling me ...

I ended the prayer wanting ...

DAY 5

WEEK #7

FOR YOUR PRAYER

PSALM 118

Practice the art of *lectio divina.*

Considering the past few days ... the past few weeks, what are you most thankful for?

Talk to God about what is on your heart.

After you are finished with your prayer, rewrite Psalm 118 in your own words on the following page.

JOURNAL

The "strongest" thought or feeling during my prayer was ...

My heart "rested" when ...

I sense the Lord was telling me ...

I ended the prayer wanting ...

Rewrite Psalm 118 in your own words.

DAY 6

WEEK #7

FOR YOUR PRAYER

JOHN 21:15-19

Practice the art of imaginative prayer

In the scene, you are Peter ... Do *you* love *Jesus*?

Would you do anything *for him*?

Would you follow *the Lord* anywhere?

Talk to God about what is on your heart.

JOURNAL

The "strongest" thought or feeling during my prayer was ...

My heart "rested" when ...

I sense the Lord was telling me ...

I ended the prayer wanting ...

Day 7

WEEK #7

FOR YOUR PRAYER

Reread your journal from weeks seven through nine

Considering the past few days … the past few weeks, what are you most thankful for?

What has God done for you?

Celebrate with Jesus and talk with Him … and listen.

JOURNAL

The "strongest" thought or feeling during my prayer was …

My heart "rested" when …

I sense the Lord was telling me …

I ended the prayer wanting …

Week Eight:

DESOLATION AND CONSOLATION

Desolation and Consolation

SESSION OUTLINE

1. "Another difficulty, especially for those who sincerely want to pray, is *dryness.* Dryness belongs to contemplative prayer when the heart is separated from God, with no taste for thoughts, memories, and feelings, even spiritual ones. ... If dryness is due to the lack of roots, because the word has fallen on rocky soil, the battle requires conversion." –CCC 2731

2. "Finally, our battle has to confront what we experience as failure in prayer: discouragement during periods of dryness ... disappointment over not being heard according to our own will; wounded pride, stiffened by the indignity that is ours as sinners; our resistance to the idea that prayer is a free and unmerited gift; and so forth. The conclusion is always the same: what good does it do to pray? To overcome these obstacles, we must battle to gain humility, trust, and perseverance." –CCC 2728

3. "I call desolation ... darkness of soul, disturbance in it, movement to low and earthly things, disquiet from various agitations and temptations, moving to lack of confidence, without hope, without love, finding oneself totally slothful, tepid, sad, and as if separated from one's Creator and Lord. For just as consolation is contrary to desolation,* in the same way the thoughts that come from consolation are contrary to the thoughts that come from desolation." –St. Ignatius of Loyola[1]

*"There are three principal causes for which we find ourselves desolate. The first is because we are tepid, slothful or negligent in our spiritual exercises, and so through our faults spiritual consolation withdraws from us. The second, to try us and see how much we are and how much we extend ourselves in his service and praise without so much payment of consolations and increased graces. The third, to give us true recognition and understanding so that we may interiorly feel that it is not ours to attain or maintain increased devotion, intense love, tears or any other spiritual consolation, but that all is the gift and grace of God our Lord, and so that we may not build a nest in something belonging to another, raising our mind in some pride or vainglory, attributing to ourselves the devotion or the other parts of the spiritual consolation." St. Ignatius of Loyola[2]

4. "Let one who is in desolation work to be in patience, which is contrary to the vexations which come to him, and let him think that he will soon be consoled, diligently using the means against such desolation, as is said in the sixth rule." –St. Ignatius of Loyola[3]

5. "We can find fresh courage for accepting with patience and faith every situation of difficulty, affliction and trial in the knowledge that from the darkness the Lord will cause a new day to dawn." –Pope Benedict XVI[4]

6. "Dear brothers and sisters, God's way of acting—very different from ours—gives us comfort, strength and hope because God does not withdraw his 'yes.' In the face of stressful human relations, even in the family, we often fail to persevere in freely given love which demands commitment and sacrifice. Instead, God does not grow tired of us; he never wearies of being patient with us and, with his immense mercy, always leads the way and reaches out to us first: his 'yes' is absolutely reliable." –Pope Benedict XVI[5]

Discussion

QUESTION #1

Describe your experience of prayer this past week.

QUESTION #2

What do you connect with as you read Saint Ignatius' description of desolation?

QUESTION #3

What do you normally do in times of desolation?
Do you feel like God is still with you during these times? Explain.

QUESTION #4

How have you grown during the past eight weeks? What have you learned through *Oremus*?

QUESTION #5

What can you do so that you continue to grow?

Day 1

WEEK #8

FOR YOUR PRAYER

LUKE 2:1-14

Practice the art of imaginative prayer.

In the scene, *you* are near the manger *with* Mary as she gives birth to Jesus.

Talk to God about what is on your heart ... and listen.

JOURNAL

The "strongest" thought or feeling during my prayer was ...

My heart "rested" when ...

I sense the Lord was telling me ...

I ended the prayer wanting ...

Day 2
WEEK #8

FOR YOUR PRAYER

LUKE 2:21-38

Practice the art of imaginative prayer.
In the scene, *you* are with Mary and Joseph as they present Jesus in the Temple.
Talk to God about what is on your heart ... and listen.

JOURNAL

The "strongest" thought or feeling during my prayer was ...

My heart "rested" when ...

I sense the Lord was telling me ...

I ended the prayer wanting ...

DAY 3

WEEK #8

FOR YOUR PRAYER

LUKE 2:41-50

Practice the art of imaginative prayer.
In the scene, you are with Mary and Joseph as they search for Jesus.
Talk to God about what is on your heart … and listen.

JOURNAL

The "strongest" thought or feeling during my prayer was …

My heart "rested" when …

I sense the Lord was telling me …

I ended the prayer wanting …

DAY 4
WEEK #8

FOR YOUR PRAYER

LUKE 2:51-52

Practice the art of imaginative prayer.
In the scene, you are with Mary and Joseph in Nazareth.
Be with Jesus as he grows in age.
Ask them to show you the hidden years of Jesus' life.
Talk to God about what is on your heart.

JOURNAL

The "strongest" thought or feeling during my prayer was ...

My heart "rested" when ...

I sense the Lord was telling me ...

I ended the prayer wanting ...

DAY 5

WEEK #8

FOR YOUR PRAYER

MATTHEW 3:13-17

Practice the art of imaginative prayer.
In the scene, *you* are Jesus in line in the river.
Listen as the Father pronounces Jesus as his beloved Son.
Ask the Father to speak those same words to *you*.
Talk to God about what is on your heart.

JOURNAL

The "strongest" thought or feeling during my prayer was ...

My heart "rested" when ...

I sense the Lord was telling me ...

I ended the prayer wanting ...

Day 6
WEEK #8

FOR YOUR PRAYER

JOHN 1:35-39

Practice the art of imaginative prayer.
In the scene, *you* are with John the Baptist.
Go to Jesus in verse 37.
"Where" does he take you in verse 39?
Talk to God about what is on your heart.

JOURNAL

The "strongest" thought or feeling during my prayer was ...

My heart "rested" when ...

I sense the Lord was telling me ...

I ended the prayer wanting ...

DAY 7

WEEK #8

FOR YOUR PRAYER

MATTHEW 4:18-21

Practice the art of imaginative prayer.

In the scene, *you* are Peter.

Jesus looks you in the eyes and asks you to follow him.

What do you say?

Talk to God about what is on your heart.

JOURNAL

The "strongest" thought or feeling during my prayer was ...

My heart "rested" when ...

I sense the Lord was telling me ...

I ended the prayer wanting ...

Some Final Thoughts from Fr. Mark Toups

"Now what? Where do we go from here?"

Perhaps you have heard those questions. Perhaps you have asked those questions. These questions echoed within the disciples in Luke, chapter 24.

Grieving Jesus' death, and worried about their future, the disciples walked "to a village named Emmaus, about seven miles from Jerusalem," (Luke 24:13). The risen Christ entered into the anxiety as he meets them along the way. While "their eyes were kept from recognizing him," their hearts "burned within" while he talked with them (see Luke 24:16, 32).

During the last eight weeks, we have shared a sacred pilgrimage. Perhaps you know the hearts of the Emmaus disciples, for perhaps you too have had your heart "burning" within. You have learned how to pray in new ways. You have grown in intimacy with Jesus, our Bridegroom. You have received direction in your spiritual life.

Now what? Where do we go from here?

Return. Saint Ignatius of Loyola would invite you to return to the moments on this journey when you have experienced God's presence the most. What meditations spoke most to you? What words enflamed your heart? What did Jesus say to you? The moments of grace that you experienced then might still be pregnant with grace for you to experience now. Returning to those meditations helps you "unpack" further what God has in store for you.

Reread your journal. Make a list of the meditations or prayer experiences that were most efficacious. Once you have your list, take time to "revisit" them one at a time. Perhaps you will spend more than one day "lingering" in the grace of a particular meditation. If so, stay there ... "sit" in the meditation for another day ... or a week ... or longer. Once the well has run dry on that particular mediation, move on to the next one that made an impact on you.

Resources. There are a few resources that may be helpful for you as you continue.

For more on praying with the Scriptures:

- *Praying Scripture for a Change: An Introduction to Lectio Divina,* by Tim Gray (Ascension Press)
- *Walking with God: A Journey Through the Bible* by Tim Gray and Jeff Cavins (Ascension Press)
- *WRAP Yourself in Scripture,* by Karen and Lawrence Dwyer (IPF Publishing), is a concise, yet packed, introduction to *lectio divina.* It is a great resource to help you deepen your experience of praying with the Scriptures.

For more on prayer and growth in holiness:

- *Communion with Christ* by Deacon James Keating (IPF Publishing)
- *Listening for Truth: Praying Our Way to Virtue* by Deacon James Keating (Liguori). This is a beautifully written invitation to grow further in the spiritual life. Essentially, once we have grown in intimacy with Christ, we should soon grow in our life of virtue. As the old spiritual sings, "Something on the inside, working on the outside, O' what change in my life!" Celebrate the "change in your life" and grow in virtue.
- *A School of Prayer* by Pope Benedict XVI (Scepter Publishers)

For more on consolation, desolation, and discerning little things:

- *The Discernment of Spirits: An Ignatian Guide for Everyday Living,* by Timothy Gallagher, O.M.V. (Crossroad) is an easy-to-read teaching on Saint Ignatius of Loyola's Rules for the Discernment of Spirits. Saint Ignatius reminds us that desolation and consolation are expected in the spiritual life. Everyone experiences desolation and consolation. The wisdom of Saint Ignatius teaches us how to respond to desolation and how to receive the fullness of consolation.
- *The Examine Prayer: Ignatian Wisdom for Our Lives Today,* by Tim Gallagher, O.M.V. (Crossroad)

Classics on the spiritual life:

- *Abandonment to Divine Providence* by Jean-Pierre de Caussade
- *The Imitation of Christ* by Thomas a Kempis
- *An Introduction to the Devout Life* by St. Francis de Sales
- *The Three Conversions in the Spiritual Life* by Reginald Garrigou-Lagrange

To learn more about Blessed John Paul II's Theology of the Body:

- *Theology of the Body for Beginners* (Ascension Press)
- *Man & Woman He Created Them: A Theology of the Body* (Pauline Books and Media)

Finally, trust that God is pursuing you. God wants you and will "tirelessly" call you to "that mysterious encounter known as prayer" (CCC 2567). The pressure is not on you. The pressure is on God. Let the Lord call you, and expect amazing things to happen.

The most important thing is to show up. Keep showing up. Stay faithful to your commitment to pray, and trust that God will do the rest.

Receive the gift of prayer.

It has been a pleasure serving you. Let's keep praying for each other.

Endnotes

A Letter from Fr. Toups

1. Pope Benedict XVI, Address of his Holiness Benedict XVI to the participants in the International Congress Organized to Commemorate the 40th Anniversary of the Dogmatic Constitution on Divine Revelation "Dei Verbum." Sept. 16, 2005.
2. Hans Urs von Balthazar, *Prayer* (San Francisco: Ignatius Press, 1986), 7.
3. *Prayer,* 7.
4. St. Therese of Lisieux, *Manuscrips autobiographiques,* C 25r.

Week One: What is Prayer?

1. Cf. *Acts* 17:27.
2. Pope Benedict XVI, General Audience, May 4, 2011
3. Hans Urs von Balthazar, *Prayer* (San Francisco: Ignatius Press, 1986), 7.
4. Pope Benedict XVI, General Audience, May 4, 2011, quoting Luke 11:1.
5. St. Ignatius of Loyola, *Spiritual Exercises #75.*
6. Pope Benedict XVI, *Deus Caritas Est,* 1.
7. Pope Benedict XVI, General Audience, May 4, 2011.
8. Pope Benedict XVI, General Audience, May 11, 2011.

Week Two: Before You Pray

1. Pope Benedict XVI, General Audience, August 3, 2011
2. Pope Benedict XVI, General Audience, August 17, 2011
3. Pope Benedict XVI, *Spe Salvi #33*
4. Pope Benedict XVI, General Audience, May 25, 2011
5. Pope Benedict XVI, General Audience, May 23, 2012
6. Saint Ignatius of Loyola, *Spiritual Exercises #48*

Week Three: ***Lectio Divina***

1. Pope Benedict XVI, Congress of Biblical Scholars, Rome, September 2005.
2. St. Teresa of Jesus, *The Book of Her Life,* 8, 5, in *The Collected Works of St. Teresa of Avila.* Tr. K.Kavanaugh, O.C.D., and O. Rodriguez, O.C.D. (Washington DC: Institute of Carmelite Studies, 1976), I, 67.
3. *Eph.* 3:16-17.

Week Four: Relational Prayer

1. Pope Benedict XVI, General Audience, June 22, 2011.
2. Pope Benedict XVI, General Audience, May 4, 2011.
3. Pope Benedict XVI, General Audience, August 10, 2011.
4. Pope Benedict XVI, General Audience, May 30, 2012.

Week Five: Spiritual Senses

1. Fr. Tim Gallagher, O.M.V., *Meditation and Contemplation* (New York: Crossroad Publishing Company, 2008), 36.

Week Six: Discernment in Prayer

1. Saint Ignatius of Loyola, *Spiritual Exercises #314,* as translated by Timothy M. Gallagher, O.M.V., in *The Discernment of Spirits* (New York: Crossroads Publishing, 2011), 7).
2. Saint Ignatius of Loyola, *Spiritual Exercises #315,* in *Discernment of Spirits,* 7.
3. Saint Ignatius of Loyola, *Spiritual Exercises #333,* in *Discernment of Spirits.*
4. Saint Ignatius of Loyola, *Spiritual Exercises #335,* in *Discernment of Spirits,* 41.

Week Seven: Dealing With Distractions

1. St. Ignatius of Loyola, *Spiritual Exercises #325.*

Week Eight: Desolation and Consolation

1. Saint Ignatius of Loyola, *Spiritual Exercises #316,* in *Discernment of Spirits,* 8.
2. Saint Ignatius of Loyola, *Spiritual Exercises #322,* in *Discernment of Spirits,* 9.
3. Saint Ignatius of Loyola, *Spiritual Exercises #321,* in *Discernment of Spirits,* 8.
4. Pope Benedict XVI, General Audience, February 22, 2012.
5. Pope Benedict XVI, General Audience, May 30, 2012.

Artwork

Week One, *The Annunciation,* by Henry Ossawa Tanner (1859-1937)

Week Two, *Creation of Adam,* by Michelangelo Buonarroti (1475-1564)

Week Three, *Song of the Angels,* by William-Adolphe Bouguereau (1825-1905)

Week Four, *Christ in the Carpenter's Shop,* by Georges de La Tour (1593-1652)

Week Five, *The Doubting of St. Thomas,* by Michelangelo Merisi Caravaggio (1571-1610)

Week Six, *The Good Samaritan,* by Jacopo Bassano (1510 - 1592)

Week Seven, *The Return of the Prodigal Son,* by Rembrandt Harmensz van Rijn (1606–1669)

Week Eight, *The Descent of the Holy Spirit,* by Anthony van Dyck (1599–1641)

Acknowledgments

I am deeply grateful to the many people whose assistance made *Oremus* possible:

I would like to thank those who taught me how to pray, namely: Rev. John Horn, SJ, president-Rector of Kenrick-Glennon Seminary in St. Louis, Missouri; Kathleen Kanavy, Director of Spiritual Director Formation for the Institute for Priestly Formation; and Rev. F. Hampton Davis III, Diocese of Lafayette. Much of *Oremus* comes from my personal experience of prayer, and I am indebted to those who were patient with me.

I would like to thank the Institute for Priestly Formation. The mission of IPF is to help priests fall in love and stay in love so that love for God determines everything in their life. God saved my life through the ministry of IPF. Furthermore, IPF taught me everything that is *Oremus*. Without IPF, *Oremus* would not be. Without IPF, my priesthood might not be. Thank you, IPF, for teaching me, forming me, and loving me. Specifically, I would like to acknowledge IPF for their articulation of "ARRR: Acknowledge, Relate, Receive, Respond." Thank you for granting permission in allowing me to share your gift of prayer.

I would like to thank Mr. Brian Butler, founder and president of Dumb Ox Productions, and Mr. Roch Gernon, also with Dumb Ox Productions, for their vision. Without them *Oremus* most likely would have remained a small project within the homes of south Louisiana. Thank you for your brotherhood and vision.

I would like to thank Matt Pinto and everyone at Ascension Press, including Steve Motyl, Patrick McCabe, Chris Cope, Heidi Saxton, Mike Fontecchio, and Stella Ziegler. Without the trust and vision of Ascension Press, *Oremus* would not be. Thank you for remaining a leader in the New Evangelization. Thank you for committing to bring the Gospel to a searching generation. In addition, I would like to thank Philip Braun for his holiness, vision, and productive expertise.

I would like to thank the Most Rev. Sam G. Jacobs, Bishop of the Diocese of Houma-Thibodaux, for his spiritual fatherhood and for encouraging me to pursue writing. I would also like to thank the Most Rev. Gregory M. Aymond, Archbishop of New Orleans, for his shepherding me when I was a seminarian, as well as for his assistance with filming within the Archdiocese of New Orleans.

I would like to thank the beautiful parishioners of St. Lucy's Catholic Church in Houma, Louisiana and St. Luke's Catholic Church in Thibodaux, Louisiana. You lured *Oremus* from my heart. It was my gift to you and now your gift is blessing others. I will always remember you with great affection.

Finally, and most importantly, I would like to thank God, the Father, "from whom every family in heaven and on earth is named" (Eph: 3:15, NAB). Thank you for your mercy, your fidelity, and your gaze. I pray that the same Father "may grant you in accord with the riches of his glory to be strengthened with power through his Spirit in the inner self and that Christ may dwell in your hearts through faith; that you, rooted and grounded in love, may have strength to comprehend with all the holy ones what is the breadth and length and height and depth, and to know the love of Christ that surpasses knowledge, so that you may be filled with all the fullness of God. Now to him who is able to accomplish far more than all we ask or imagine, by the power at work within us to him be glory in the church and in Christ Jesus to all generations, forever and ever. Amen," (Eph 3:16-21, NAB).